I0210889

WINTERREISEN

ALAN HALSEY
&
KELVIN CORCORAN

KFS

Newton-le-Willows

Published in the United Kingdom in 2019
by The Knives Forks And Spoons Press,
51 Pipit Avenue,
Newton-le-Willows,
Merseyside,
WA12 9RG.

ISBN 978-1-912211-47-0

Copyright © Alan Halsey & Kelvin Corcoran, 2019.

The right of Alan Halsey & Kelvin Corcoran to be identified as the authors of this work has been asserted by them in accordance with the Copyrights, Designs and Patents Act of 1988. All rights reserved. No part of this publication may be reproduced, stored in a retrieval system, transmitted in any form or by any means, electronic, photocopying, recording or otherwise, without prior permission of the publisher.

Acknowledgements:

All images by Alan Halsey.

'The comedian steps up' was first published in *Molly Bloom*, 'The choir included some familiar faces' and 'In the days of Lee Harwood' in *Intercapillary Space* and *Winterreisen* II in *e.ratio*. Kelvin Corcoran's contributions to 'In the days of Lee Harwood' and the poem beginning 'Iain Guido Smith ...' appeared in his *Article 50*, Longbarrow Press 2018. Our thanks to the editors.

Supported using public funding by

ARTS COUNCIL ENGLAND

LOTTERY FUNDED

Contents

I: 2015-16

The comedian steps up

K: He was telling the one about
the old Byzantine test for heresy;
break his arms and legs, chuck him in the Bosphorus:
if he floats fine, if he sinks fine, there's your answer.

He was telling the one about the great divide
on Paynim shore as a way of speaking the sentence
containing the word Apokatastasis, come on you dolts,
metamorphose into something better.

He was telling the one about
what you can do with a loose mouth running
strung like a rubber band around an absence
you know, sucking in the world to save it.

He was etc – see, this is my mouth behind my mouth
for me to talk out of turn out of time
the acoustic boom off this wall like hell
stone-tongue clapper trap by the grace of God.

And with that mouth I say

I would not play light with the mother
Lady of the Way, Hodegetria
the inner knowledge   and the outer
show us the way   restore the city.

A: To wait 24 thousand years
for the ekpyrosis
only to return as what I was,
a one-man double-act.

Damn you Chrysippus.
My name in Greek means
the-Ern-who-swallowed-Eric
also translated as
self-contemplating Zeus,

ha, miching Malachi,
I'd call it self-disgusted
if they'd let me. All I ever
asked was some restitution
then along came St Peter
then that Philip with his
'image which must enter
through the image' which
I reckoned was a bridal suite
in a 5-star hotel with
the faux-classic décor of
the Origen franchise.

What's that you said? –
the lady in the third row
with the Hammurabi T-shirt –
were you shouting 'Luther'?
That devil who declared
comic actors are the wrong
kind of devil? Do you
take me for a Dimbleby?
Here in MediaCity often
misread as Mendacity
Question Time's in
the studio next door.

K: And question time is always everywhere
so I dreamt the big ninety-five
hammered to the door in a myth
just to land this shit, as misread theses
and make way for Science.

Thus the law of Hammurabi
recorded the first nuclear formula
righteousness a mighty weapon
or soft mediation of the unpalatable
I don't believe a word of it.

In the ditch next door the liars
we let run our business go oink
and the woman was shouting lustre
or lecher and no-one blushed
under a 5-star sky Dante was appalled.

A: Don't get me going,
you've heard my Vita Nuova routine,
I can't do it any more,
it depended on Beatrice being under-age.
Now they want me to pretend
she was a proper grown-up woman.
You'd be blinder than Homer not to see that
the bit where they arrive in Paradiso
with all those saints rubbernecking for a shufty
would lose half its stuffing.
Okay okay the make-up department
could doll her up as not quite sixteen,
old enough in some annals
to have been twice widowed
which only goes to show
historians can tell it as it was and is.
That's what I should have been
as my dad always said but
getting back to Dante how about an Inferno
or at least Circle 8 Ditch 8 starring
Iain Duncan Smith as Chief Guy Forked Tongue,
just say the word and tell me when.

K: Iain Guido Smith did make division and gather the spoils
plied his bonny craft the Centre for Social Justice far,
tacking across the lake of fire all the way to Betsygate.

Then setting fires in Baghdad and Washington and London,
his smug little face caressed by the claw of the Lady Margaret,
he conspired in the smoky arts of a sovereign nation once again.

The image, which must enter through the image, deserted him
his stand-up was only comical when he tried for gravitas
his mirage bucket for storing mirage history had a fuck hole in it.

But as certain creatures can live on air in hope of future meat
his tongue flickered pinkly as the girl Europa struggled all at sea,
sweet she was and pretty as live bait foundering on the shore.

Can such scenes be used by proper grown-up men to have their way?
Can drowned children's limbs be arranged to spell Breakthrough Britain?
Guido stoops to gather his spoils and build a new nation for old time's sake.

A: Are you okay in the back row
or should we call in the medics?
I'd take the lot of you home
if I didn't think you're all asylum-seekers.
Yes that always gets a roomful of chortles,
you must love yourselves bitterly
to come to stand-up. Shout when I've
gone too far so I'll know I haven't
gone far enough. Have you ever wondered
how many people have died laughing?
I was making a list but lost count and you can't
always tell the odds between humour and horror.
That's the thing about this strawman Smith
or that Jackanapes Straw – remember him?
All right, let's turn up the volume and unite or die,
it's time for the finale of this famous celebration
and for me to put a match to our
blow-me-up Betsy of a benefit bonfire
punningly labelled, in case anyone
still hasn't got it, Mt Purgatory.

K: I fell asleep on the train speeding through a long tunnel
under that mountain those invasive voices came in close
dedicated to their own preferment on the middle air.

I dreamt there was a Tory government and didn't know the place,
heard dictation from the mirage book of history in self-effacing chorus
for instance: Troy fell on Damascus, became a logical assumption.

They live in high towers above the river, sparky sparky they circulate
corporate ghosty men and women spin spin in golden circles
from the radiant centrifuge they measure the bounce in system collapse.

For instance: you can lead a horse to water even in the desert
but it's easier to perform a miracle than speak straight in such times
and the times don't change and they know it and lead on by rote.

In their archaeology of long occupation the dust of fallen capitals
rises over our heads and shows how even Jerusalem fell upon itself,
Jerusalem the Golden made dumb with a mouthful of ash.

They were having
a right old barney

K: And that's what it looks like
though it may be entirely metaphysical
or about poetry even
overbearing, dark and insistent
the condition of poiesis.

The more he said, the less it meant
– just shut up and get out
for your words, your craft
in an odourless spray
has turned to shit.

I think it was the missing thought
between them made for the fight,
beyond the academy of stipends
they barked and gestured
school school anti-school.

Syntax of burnt branches denatured
will not support thought
will not free the fucking people;
and that's what it looks like
bereft of the real classical, the human.

A: It all started when André Breton
called Tristan Tzara an impostor.
After Man Ray backed Tzara
Breton trashed the furniture and
Francis Picabia said 'Quite right too'.
When the filth arrived Breton
called Tzara a grass and punched
the daylights out of his friend
Yvan Goll. It wasn't long before
Picabia was badmouthing Breton
but none of this was proletarian
enough for Louis Aragon who
signed up with the Commies who

called Breton a Trot. Then Roger
Gilbert-Lecomte had something
to say. We thought no one ever
listened to that smackhead but
that may have been why Breton
laid down the law with his
degrees of moral competence
and somebody made him
a crown of thorns for his trouble.
You can imagine what a barney
there was after that. It was a way
people had of having fun in Paris.

K: Then the circus moved onto New York
by the law of unintended consequences,
back-wash splatter pop pulled the poets in
to play the main-chance out of the loft
and scoop CIA funds for the avant-garde.

That's how we had fun in times moderne
male and muscular shot the shit up the Ivans,
better than a dose of ICBMs;
the New York chapter besieged Berlin,
the future hammered out on that anvil.

Picabia, Breton, Tzara, the whole gang
drank heavy drafts of irrelevance juice,
joined the Foreign Legion to see the desert,
sleep under the stars, sip tea, arm wrestle
and compile the Encyclopaedia.

A Absinthe. Appropriation. (see culture)
B Bebop. Beckett. (see culture)
C Co-opted. Culture. (see culture)

D was to be for desert, culture of,
but there was nothing in it for them;

the empty quarter resumed its majesty,
the Shamal, the Simoom, the Rashabair
said you're not so smart, said nothing at all.

A: But isn't this the point about Automatic Writing,
that you can't really claim anybody wrote it?
So when one starts calling the other one a plagiarist,
says for example
'You're much too little to write such big words' –

There are anyway several versions of all these stories,
including the fate of the Encyclopaedia.
Some say it was completed, some that they actually saw it,
printed on one of those papers they fetishised,
Hollande van Gelder or Maillol or Madagascar or Japon Imperial
depending on who you believe. Bound in full calf,
edges gilt, engravings throughout, 26 volumes A-Z
(K, X and Z were the most extensive),
edition of a single copy signed by all contributors.
And they had it there in the marquee that night
they reckoned somebody cheated at Exquisite Corpses.
When they'd flung all the ashtrays at each other's heads
the only missiles they had left were –
you don't need all the details, you can guess.
And you can probably guess
who snuck out under the tentflap when nobody was looking
with A-C in his rucksack.

K: Automatic biting's all the same:
it's personal enough, you'll know who did it
because their face will be next to the teeth
buried in your arm, leg, stomach, arse etc.

The Big Word Company never really delivered,
neither world advantage nor compensation;
taking pot-shots in the long library for laughs,
was a bit Bullingdon, hand weavers the lot of them.

It came down to the texture of the vellum
upon which the words were laid as law,
talk about reification as the nation goes gaga,
talk about 80,000 smacks for their placebo.

The entries omitted, unrecorded were obvious:
no knowledge can ever be private unless stolen;
class loyalty trumps all else in the game of top tribes;
you're telling me you didn't make up those names?

The choir included
some familiar faces

K: The choir were not as one about the history
of the singing alphabet wherever it arose
and shared no consensus descant or no
on disputes across the Pontic steppes:
forgive me horsemen of the endless sky
I haven't a clue what you're saying.

This face hammered into a clay tablet
sparked a different branch entirely,
a divergence in phonics turned fatal
and made for repeated border raids
for women, cattle, any useful shit to hand;
the little triangle said it all – you don't mean?

Fishman, Stoneman, Shieldman dance
beat out your song on the wires of the world
beat out your semantic pulses unreformed
like birds in the wilderness down in Demerara;
survey the sea of grass, the predawn cities;
the rippling light, message after message arrives.

So, through time in the yoyo sport of civilisation
the choir came to include unfamiliar faces too;
and you horseman riding straight as an arrow
full tilt before the breaking wave of polyphony,
black feathers in your hair, stand in a circle and sing:
everything is there, for you the stones arrayed speak.

A: In those spaces
between words
sung and heard

Wire knot a swan
where rivers rose
sense scant as air

Liar liar
growl the basses
lower and lower

Let least
lack less
castrati trill

Every one
of those flinty
shrill sopranos

is an auntie of
one or more of
the Sultan's wives

K: The Sultan's mind grasped
    the law of succession, the neat garrotte
    a case of blades, the sherbet airs of Spring.

    The singing was peripheral but welcome
    as accompaniment to the sex riot,
    those voices rising to the casement a river.

    A river running back to Anatolia
    the Ottoman hegemony mint-fresh
    to make the whole world his private garden.

    The Sultan's mind grasped many things
    all thought is thought about something
    there were no abstractions.

    Quarter tones left open tiny doors
    through which the mind could slip
    to think the unthinkable unknown blank

    Such that when sense escapes ellipses
    the empire is in decline, the choral voices
    unfamiliar were not as one about history.

Oh horseman return like flame
a wave across the singing steppe
free of lies the old song of blood.

A: As it happened the strangers from the steppe –
five men and two women – arrived on foot.
'But your horses' we protested: 'hour after hour
we've listened to your horses approaching.'

The strangers smiled and began their audition.
Then those distant horses rose from their throats,
came galloping out between closed teeth,
drumming down to the river, whinnying skyward.

Your Highness: This is the reason
you will see some unfamiliar faces,
and hear the music they call 'clear sound',
on our return to Court.

K: So the ghost riders of the East
set about the party with horsehead fiddle
and Tuuvan throat ballads
a season-long performance.

The absent horses were there
a thunderous seismic signature
wave after wave of votive horses
shaking the court to dust, they sang

we don't fall into your story telling
nor end in a ditch or skirmish
for a lost literary convention
sealing the mouth of a lost people etc.

The strangers knew about history
came ready for it, armed to the teeth
with an oral tradition sharp as a knife
they were of one mind and they triumphed.

A: One sang five thousand verses
every night for seven nights.
We heard his hero descend
into the world of the changelings –

in our minds' eyes we saw him
fight to the death Earth Belly,
Three Shadows and the Yelping Maiden.
We trembled at the terrible cunning

of Famous Snake and Sir Bloodclot –
how fortunate his horse had warned him
with such wise words! And then his sister
disguised as a bird with a golden tail

divided in eight branches. They tell this
of Nyurgan Bootur the Quick Slinger.
We will say more of the Three Worlds
in a further despatch to Your Highness.

K: ' . . . the manners of mankind do not differ so widely as our voyage
writers would make us believe. Perhaps it would be more entertaining to add
a few surprising customs of my own invention; but nothing seems to me so
agreeable as truth.'

There's the three world escalator hop-stop;
Well, it's hardly unique phenomenology said Tammuz,
try these little axes planted in my chest for Spring
and think of Orpheus, his double-take, fatal,
then, after all that, it's goodbye singing head Beach Boy.

But well, ok, in the end – the three worlds waiting,
Mary Wortley Montagu's telegram explained it all:
why the singers did not return to court,
why a mythology can wear out its welcome,
how a moment of direct observation refutes the lot.

Your Highness, forgive my digressions, my unnaming,
fish   shield   big fish   manface   perhaps a boat.
If we return by descent to that first picture
dot   dot   dash   your swift reply is awaited
by zoomorphic grapheme with holes drilled in pebbles.

Fish   shield   big fish   manface   river boat
ready to be slung like stars around Quick Slinger's neck,
that would be his real neck in a fable – that sort of anatomy,
and the picture remains unread though familiar
returned by descent, the song lasts only one season.

In the days of Lee Harwood

K: A trail of bookmarks, a trail of postcards
    I found around the house after you left
    tick tack toe through the little labyrinth
    a string of shining beads in a lost currency
    and his many different faces came and went
    in the days of the days of Lee Harwood.

    Poet most alive living nowhere now
    clues come fluttering from the shelves,
    late arrivals from not the full story,
    that walk we never made across the Downs
    Grasscut CD 1 inch ½ mile, map and voices
    drilling holes in the discontinued calendar.

A: (The Sinking Colony Revisited)

    'The inventory seemed endless'
    but I'll return to that. It wasn't something
    we talked of at the time, my young wife and I.
    Nor did we discuss the aims of the Raj
    and she never referred to the department reports
    she must have known even then I hadn't sent.
    And yet on the evenings (many as I now remember)
    when the musicians despite their promises
    failed to appear on our verandah
    we talked and talked, very often of our recurrent
    apparently synchronised dreams of the Arctic.
    Moose, snow shoes, sledge, yes the inventory again
    but not the one I mean to reconsider.
    It was a rare evening one of us neglected to mention
    our feeling we had never left the base camp,
    our bungalow down in the foothills. There we were
    in the mountains, in our 'mansion set in magnificent grounds'
    with the latest agricultural machinery, dehumidifiers,
    heavy iron gates … yet in our minds we were
    still in the lowland with binoculars trained on
    those faraway peaks. But the inventory, the other one …

'Printing press', not stating it was old as Aldus.
'Pig (logo)', whatever that meant in those days.
'Cauldron with flowers', make of that what you will.
'Road map', of England, no use to us.
'Calendar' as my friend writes 'discontinued'
but then of future date. 'Portrait of young lady
with floral hat', which prompted me to ask
'Haven't we been here before?' –
my young wife, not in white as in the poem
but in 'fancy dress'? No, as she was, at another time.

K: This was all so but from another time
   the reminders kept arriving, the paths not taken beckoned,
   that secluded bay in the heat of the afternoon
   after the rains finished and a translucent curtain opened
   across the whole vista of their other ways.
   And though the scheme was for the benefit of all,
   the metropolis and the dominions let's say,
   there was a groundswell and unexpected events;
   the radicalisation of the tennis club,
   the close down of the baking circle,
   the preference for autochthonic dance.

   Your soft linen like a wing swept the verandah
   analogous to the mystery of the rain-washed view,
   another season of calculations, of glad-handing
   the nabobs and salesmen, their butterfly wives.
   At least the women set the air alight, a sort of flagrance.
   I never knew if it was sex or absent-mindedness,
   lost deep in the intricacies of the local dialect
   itself a version of an implacable, closed book,
   it might as well have been shapes scratched on rock
   or pitter-patter feet around the bay for all I grasped,
   I just never knew and none of us saw it coming.
   I like to think our expeditions were genuine,
   were not always for cover but for pure geology.

Later I learnt Captain Harwood's reports were correct,
they predicted the whole thing – you just couldn't tell,
he was so unassuming, gentle in his detachments,
and the reports were filed in Government House,
under a heading of *Fanciful Imaginings At Large*.
I suppose the engine of the age can run on,
can drive every detail of our lives and loyalties
and we don't talk about it, we just don't see it
and I came to think that's because we're inside it
encompassed and blind, duty-bound, modern.
I still thought this when she left for England,
that she had failed, fallen into a character flaw,
and I lay there every night under vague imaginings
pretty ghosts circling the mosquito net, entwined
low susurrations of an erotic folk literature
released from their red mouths all night.

I must close, be done, you have been very patient,
there's no final account and the inventory continues,
a delivery of leather buckets for the collection of Yak milk,
wrongly dispatched, bullets of incorrect calibre,
non-regulation dubbing, polo mallets and hegemony cranks.
All I can do is wait for the cargo boat to arrive
let it edge its way into the bay without reprisal,
I doubt they even know the name of this place.

A: 'And that,' he murmured, shutting the album,
    'was what my great-uncle told me
    forty years ago.' Then to break
    what to me felt too long a silence
    but to him was a necessary pause
    anyone might fill more gracefully than I:
    'So when the cargo boat finally arrived
    he came back to his house on the Downs,
    to his wife?'
            He crossed the room,
    stood looking out of that floor-to-ceiling window,

in that way he had of seeming to belong
to an age much friendlier than ours, eyes fixed
on that steepest of streets reaching down to the seafront,
the shocking dazzle of the late summer sun on the water,
children skimming pebbles on the incoming tide,
three tankers on the skyline heading east
towards the Strait.
                    'The address she sent him
didn't exist. He heard later that she'd changed her name.
Bigamy, perhaps. They never met again.'

K: Trail of postcards to nowhere then, unaddressed
    straight through the winding Platonic streets;
    England crouches, its back turned to the continent
    resentful, effaces history and dreams an America;
    despite this you can see the sea from Brunswick Place
    and poetry leaps at the high windows then,
    you meet an old friend go to a bar and the stars appear.

    Take the scenes connected over the years in turn,
    each one designed by Donald Evans open and at rest:
    poet and old friend, the years relived in one night;
    poet tackles bank robber, receives public acclaim;
    poet in a foreign city at one, making it his home;
    poet in labyrinth turns, follows the sound of the sea;
    poet scales the final mountain, everyone's there, it's ok.

II: 2016-17

At last there was some
News from Daddland

K: The news was not new, it was
  rust bloom on the basilica chewing faith,
  for all your pretty shape it is
  the shitty lid of a manhole cover graced
  by grass, a dead-end in thought, Daddland
  sucked down the dark tunnel at last.

A: It was the judge's third case of patricide
  in the last six months, unless he dreamed it.
  Artists, he'd concluded, are a danger to society,
  generally speaking. Because they never doubt
  where dreams are concerned. Or because
  they think dreams are always concerned.

K: He was having second thoughts, the green
  gone purple before his first thought ended,
  his faith in transliteration bruised
  for a song of the vetches and innocent grass;
  jump out of your ditches my bonny fellows
  and never dream where doubts are sown.

A: 'Tell the great Osiris I have done the deed
  which is to set him free' – but then again
  'I didn't – no gammon – I tell you I shan't –
  only stabbed him once.' It's the tense confusion,
  mask slipping off focus, remorseless grave bulbs
  springing up among the bloated windfalls.

K: Yes, I'll tell the old boy your news,
  though I have a locker-full of limbs,
  last time I checked, the requisite number,
  dancing the day, though the sun ate my mind,
  though my head's turned backwards, and I think
  too long on the preservative qualities of sand.

A: Dazed among daisies, easy as the day
    puts horns on his head he comes on like
    a feller with stage fright, fraughtest of stags,
    sunstruck apple stuck in his gob. Logger beware
    he's sizing you up all ready to lob into the big
    bad world where good goblins shouldn't go.

K: Dazed among daisies, graced on grass
    his scampering step timed to a fruit bowl brain,
    the chemistry of which is not fully understood;
    we people it with demons in a dark wood.
    Come out of that, taste candid kind of apple flesh,
    the chemistry of Eden made plain as day.

A: As transparent as scripture turned
    this way and that until it's brainless
    as a mummy, all mystery sucked out
    but scarcely missed. Step on it, scamp,
    hurry home to Memphis before time's up
    and you're flung to the press, heart in ferment.

K: Which is why they're called Originalists,
    to impart a living truth to a foxed document,
    a moment in time, hallowed and untouchable.
    Yet they aspire to their constitution and spin,
    if there was a history of ideas, we'd be against it.
    The words unwrite themselves and a house burns.

A: It was rightly named, that house of correction.
    The inmates rush out to watch the doctored files
    flaming skyward, nicely massaged accounts,
    revised witness statements, waterboard confessions,
    gone with the obtuse messages of secret poems
    and paintings of the netherworld in obscene detail.

Cracking the code
proved impossible

K: I won't engage with it, the terminology
of codes and decipherment is inadequate,
I got to use words to talk to you,
my big bad thumbprint smack on your forehead
and that giant lurks in etymology,
at least there's a science to explain all this.

A: I hear you Sweeney crying out loud
in some footnote, wiping your thumbs
on that grease-monkey T-shirt with the
'I was there' motto. Some virtual maze
you brag you invented. You Agonistes
me Janus. Etymology my arse.

K: As it turns out these bones do speak,
etymology my elbow, even beyond Proto-Germanic;
diet, trauma and muscle formation for instance,
a literal life hand-in-glove with the *oikumene;*
agon – whether you fancy the fight or no,
up now Sweeney – off your tump and at it.

A: And what do we see – can you believe that's
Sweeney reconfigured as a very early bird
just recently awarded his singular plumage?
But no. He looks more like Lord Tennyson
fresh from the grave with a mouthful of slogans,
an Isle of Wight separatist, a most political poet.

K: Those islanders were wedded to the dead, the wrong dead,
their grave dribblings, their sucking mouths,
whilst pedalling in reverse at full-tilt into darkness.
From that advantage point they held firm beliefs;
for instance, they could make the world revolve backwards
and meet their younger selves on the road to Freshwater.

A: To the white tower they came, the sparkling new Gothic,
the first sight they had of Dimbola Lodge. Here they sat
for Mrs Cameron, for her long exposures in soft focus,
got the fidgets while she fiddled with wet plates. Some
here became King David, Beatrice Cenci, Queen Guinevere.
Note also the distant statue of Mr Hendrix the guitarist.

K: Hendrix took flight all the way from Seattle,
Jimi Jimi, get on the bus and take the wheel
but even singers die – and it's gratuitous.
I.M. all you like, lacustrine nimbus mourner,
the long home lodge is now a museum and gallery
abandoned in a locked green labyrinth.

A: Probably Lord T didn't write the reportedly
lost poem beginning 'All along the watchtower'
but his was a time to search copse and dell for beings
only cameras could see. Ours to unearth hidden faces
in album covers. To forget that photos do lie.
That no snaps are memories but some memories snap.

K: The princes kept the view and sucked up big data,
that history is but the trail of snap snapped memories
we stumble on in the dark wood damp with seasonal rot.
Then to the White Tower we came, the nation's theme park;
children ride half price into a future, almost allegory,
launched into the night, a social contract revoked.

A: Poor Jean-Jacques, struck off the guest list,
shambles through that wood, out to pick mushrooms
and finding none. 'Autumn these days', he grumbles,
'has also been lost in translation'. And whatever happened
to those children? The ghost train came back empty.
That future was a past a wicked quarterwit imagined.

Compared to a
late Roman copy

K: It was the goddess Labrys in her labyrinth
everywhere and nowhere to be found,
it's hard to get your mouth around it;
linguistic drift westward buried her
awash on the shores of Cumae in season
– Oh Labrys, Most Holy, show us the way in/out.

A: What kind fortune some of us
have eyes in the backs of our heads
or else we'd've missed the four
sheer white columns of Aphrodite's temple
towering above that wine-bright sea.
More fizz for everyone around this table.

K: Aphrodite came swanning out of a milky sea,
this was Cyprus and I was young in whiteness
– as for fizz, plenty of that on the waves,
turned to fuzz now, the eyes you see don't,
their evolution is poor and incomplete;
the temple was buried in a green grove shining.

A: There's no counting how many drowned
on that crossing, crying prayers to a god
none of our people had heard of or from.
Some point to evidence that Cupid survived
while some rejoice at the mysterious purpose
they're told Mister Big still keeps up his sleeve.

K: The watery trench between two continents
undid our sailing kind for centuries, that fault
all settled now, no-one drowns for a better life,
riding the subduction zone is peaceful by comparison;
Africa nudges Europe, more than hints a vengeful god,
says we're a late Roman copy razing Carthage.

A: So we claim that permission, that imposition,
to love Empire to the point of abhorrence.
Those offices, labyrinthine lairs of insurance men,
lawyers, bailiffs and experts in tax evasion
we prefer to forget and forget they reflect
in their flaws and fissures the tenements of saints.

K: Which left me lurking in an ante-chamber
tip-toeing around their hushed adamantine rule,
at the door they know your name and barely nod
settle you sweetly in the ways of abhorrence.
There's a mechanism for amnesia and its franchise,
we're contracted to it, a shining city on a hill.

A: Then we all fall down and Hollywood rewrites us.
Here's your cute squaddie's skirt, try these leggy sandals:
today you're a slave who must pretend to revolt.
Just don't snigger when you see the new emperor,
the halfwitted one with the flyaway thatch, he's for real.
Remember to say 'Rome is great again', silly as it sounds.

K: The tenement of saints is just along the road
favoured by pigeons, a domestic economy
kept off the books, they built no lasting city.
The tenement of saints stands unoccupied,
the insouciance men run it as a populist coup
but accounts don't record a fake empire.

A: But where else could we buy fake-me shoes?
We wanted felicity but got facility instead.
We heard about massacres that never happened
and so proved our safety. We learnt the perils
of 'so' in 'society' 'solecism' 'sovereignty'
'soft' 'soap' 'soteriology' and good old 'sop'.

They'd Overlooked Several
Other Clues to the Structure

K: I'd say they'd overlooked the whole thing
seeing nothing in another pile of Structuralist voodoo,
another minus zero terminology I can't abide.
I'd say echo sound location made the picture
and the picture talked first capitals, first inscription
a point of origin incarnate holding the centre.

A: I've heard it claimed that the 'point of origin'
referred to an agent who held the centre with
a 1950s army issue rifle. The Structuralists
filched the idea from a sitcom treatment
of Dante's *Inferno*, a long-forgotten flop.
As for echo location a pipistrelle would know.

K: The same old gang of apparatchiks sat on the roof,
rule book and Kalashnikovs to hand, idlers for hire,
dreaming how to fuzz up the image wall, just fat babies
bouncing down Dante's Funfair helter-skelter
to arrive at the means of production without a clue,
Is this a spanner or a hermeneutic paradox?

A: It's likely a sap in an early film noir
ripe for deconstruction. Artfully applied
it k.o.'s the hero, ensuring that the plot
can unfold without him for some untold time.
But the apparatchiks neglect to bring him round
and tell their boss he's as dead as any author.

K: Roland Barthes jumps out of a cab at The Continental,
he's here to wash our eyes and rinse the pictures,
dreaming of Jacques Derrida on a tank come to set us free.
But all of this was before the invention of radar,
so what shapes our thought about it, forwards and backwards,
traces to a living source unknown I've only heard in song.

A: We hear it still in 'Who Killed Cock Robin?'
I, said the laundryman. I, said his van.
Who saw him die? I, said the fisheye
they'd fixed to the tank. I, said the ground
as it sank beneath him. Who heard his last words?
I, said the bleep radar hears in its sleep.

K: The digital reduction of that stream
suggests a sort of music, though not dance hall.
So we stood around him, attendant and clueless,
to see the read-out slow slow, bleep a stop;
no-one stepped forward to assume his place,
time will deal with that, said the consultant.

A: Wise words. All the faculty members
attending this pre-breakfast symposium
claim they are the rightful heirs although
with due respect as politicians say
they beg to differ. Okay beg. Okay differ.
Just show me the way to the canteen.

K: Just show me the way to go home,
the way to the garden and a beer, thank you.
Surround me with banks of waving digitalis,
steady my heart and let me hear their tiny bells ringing.
Show me the silver lights of the glowing circuit
and let me know it for the first time.

A: Meanwhile back at the symposium
they're busy listing films to be shown
in Plato's Cave. Either I'm dreaming or
your head's spinning round. Now So-&-So's
unravelling the ins & outs of Yeats's
widening gyres and now we know we know.

They Set Out ...

K: They set out for the Pole the next morning
the fur of their parka hoods curtains of ice,
'Hup hup', said Roald, making music of the air
and the dogs bounding to the source of chill,
to magnetic north of exact degree, our bones, I said
I was freezing when I was a head.

A: I sometimes thought that when I was a head
I was had. That bastard who tried to tear
up the photos was probably the one who'd
so carelessly entangled the rigging. Luckily
he hanged himself – 'inadvertently' we said and
pressed on. In those days there seemed no bounds.

K: His word objects dropped from the air
taking their form from the sound at last
to imprint themselves on the hidden ground.
'Hup Hup', said the Alan, setting out afresh
and the powdered snow raised their shape
into the blue zero of our boundless days.

A: I did as I was told, set those brittle twigs
in the ice in clumsy remembrance of our 3-master.
We still trusted their promise of a rescue party –
people who would not mistake VV for W
or, much worse, M. Is memory really
a red filter? Not dear old sepia or cyan tone?

K: Ah that's poets talking to poets, the live and the dead
yammer yammer in those empty crowded crevasses,
up there that slow dance red blotch a fool's fire
and we see the underside of their big word HELP
it opens its empty mouth at the empty sky
our footprints eaten as red signal memory falls away.

A: 'And' – as the words come back – 'sinks in its traces'
which base camp took to mean we dug out of the crevasse
smashed china, cups, plates and shards of fine glass,
a treasure to some and evidence at last of the dwellings
in that most happy land. O Ta Neter! O Hyperborea! O Sumeru!
O and more fools they, gulled yet again by ordinary language.

K: And what they found can finally be explained;
a wealth of evidence poured into her lap,
the objects of a language to hand newly made,
stone-tools, blades, cups and tiny goddesses,
the Arctic as the last thought of the G-d leaving
– and look, that's a ship amidst the bergs and fog.

A: Where the ice is receding and nervous
grubby bears jump newsprung rivers. Looks like
there's been a gamma ray burst not so many
light years away and there's iron-60 just
below ground level. Then they start to bicker
about words and names and territorial rights.

K: You could surely build an empire on this lot,
silvery white cerium, scandium and chutzpah
and that neodymium in your ear speaks my voice.
Prices are indicative in our warehouses in Rotterdam
and there's no dispute over rights, see this whiphand;
they fell from the sky for us to build an empire.

A: Landed on earth with a bundle of handbooks
to ensure the jargon would be understood.
Look here's a whole bloody library all yours
if you don't mind soggy paper. The books float
down the gullies past the nonplussed bears,
pages flip in the current then slowly detach.

III: 2017-18

1.1

'Yet war in the sense of an organised campaign … is unknown to primitive societies and seems, like capitalism, slavery, class distinctions, specialised professions, and urban civilisation to be a development of the Neolithic revolution.'

— Maurice Bowra, *Primitive Song*

K: In the second year of the Ikea riots
　　Government as Vision Divestment Corp
　　reconfigured the relations of men and women;
　　edict 1: Don't Say I Don't Do Anything For You.

A: Edict 2: Don't Say That Was Easy If It Never Was.
　　Archaeologists excavating the Anthropocene epoch
　　report a sudden decimation of stationery shops
　　cotemporaneous with the hermaphrodites' coup d'état.

K: Well there's head and there's head,
　　how did they ever talk to each other back then?
　　Back then, like now, causal and casual consort
　　and my little trowel scrapes at the difference.

A: Distances then were measured in parsecs
　　so they had to shout. What a comical
　　row they used to make, what a cosmic racket,
　　back in the days before war broke out.

K: Gravitational waves impressed in foam rubber,
　　real surroundsound rib-ticklers for the survivors,
　　left imprints of the faces of diverse figures
　　Putin, Murdoch, Tamburlaine in their dotage.

A: Edict 3: Don't Forget Him Even When He's Gone.
China called Mugabe their All-Weather Friend
until they checked their accounts. $5bn new investment
if the generals would slightly adjust the gravitation.

K: What does it matter? All-weather friend, all-weather pitch.
We can't feed people Astroturf, they can't eat that and work;
intellectual property so disbursed won't fit my rucksack,
a new face at the tent flap, a debt called in centuries later.

A: Even Nebuchadnezzar will give up when Astroturf's all
there's left to chew. Then figures will show full employment
and no matter nobody's been paid. When Astroturf
runs out you'll find good nutrition in plastic empties.

K: War – what is it good for? It's good for trade and darkness,
the darkness we fall into, the trampoline of plastic empties.
Edict 4: a generation later write an identikit family history,
be applauded by spoon-fed liberals, oh my exile etc.

A: So we trace our descent: Uncle X served
in Y Regiment, great-uncle too, but his granddad
got tarred & feathered. The same granddad whose
brother cut some jolly smart deals in the Congo.

K: As Casement said to Conrad sitting in Matadi,
such things cannot be forgotten,
ten million deaths cannot be forgotten,
copper, cobalt, diamonds, cannot be forgotten.

A: Casement should know, hanged in Irish minds in
the present continuous while Croke Park's strafed
by the Black & Tans, a local told me in Dublin
as if it had happened that afternoon, April 1986.

K: Living history wrote the ballad of Roger Casement
but some men live their times like Leopold II,
like Cromwell in Drogheda. You want a job, try mine,
said the curator of the Museum of African History, Brussels.

A: 'A job? A job?' groaned the Grand Old Poet,
'Living History Incarnate, that's job enough for me'.
Then he chanted 'The Curse of Cromwell'
in his Voice of the Bard and the sidhe made merry.

K: Shut up: grand old poets are paid to groan,
look at Wordsworth, we turned him lickety-split;
Blake blamed Homer for all the wars of Europe
and Marvell was merely blatant in the Ode.

A: The poets shuffle out, bloody-eyed,
back to their caves in the anthologies
half a mile north of Neglect,
watched by Eng. Lit. lads on CCTV.

1.2

'Chang E, wife of the fox-hunting Lord Yi, is supposed to have stolen the herb of immortality from her husband and fled to the moon, where she turned into a toad.'

— David Hawkes, *The Songs of the South*

A: Frogs have always seemed a happy bunch
and only superstition's worried by the moon.
But toads? Thumbs down. They don't jump
they crawl. They'd be OK if they weren't so human.

K: No doubt chlorine washed under cellophane.
No doubt a ball of the brutes fucking in a puddle.
I want I want, she said ascending moonlit stairs,
rinsing the thought of his squat, inhuman genitals.

A: Ah Chang E, Chang E, you've left the ladder in place.
Mr Blake clambers up and stands beside her.
They gawp and tremble. Neither had expected to find
that rant of a flag with the stars and stripes.

K: Blake stippled the print with ashes of flags,
powdered the still lakes of Far Province.
Oh say can't you see a series of rhetorical questions?
Redface the fox all-knowing stepped into cover.

A: Redface probably reckons Lord Yi will be next
up the ladder with his horn & his hounds
sniffing those deep lunar shadows. Listen to me,
Redface: these are studio shots, you're not in the picture.

K: Not in the picture proved a form of lethal nostalgia;
the ladder was crowded, pull it up, pull it up, that old trick.
Lethal nostalgia on my left and on my right,
hand-in-hand we backed into the Taklamakan Desert.

A: Veered south from the Celestial Mountains
and the dear old stretches of the Silk Road.
Here's where Lord Yi's clan bagged the last tiger,
where Redface's brothers pad round the oil wells.

K: The Caspian depression is a bargain basement,
don't think deep blue sea or Silk Road rendered;
the chemistry of bitumen has a lot to answer for
since it was used to stick together the bricks of Babylon.

A: The chemistry of bitumen foxed the painters,
their pigments corrupt, their crafty suntints
turn foul green then black. But this statuette's
made of the same, bright as day: the buxom Chang E.

K: Of course the moon: 嫦娥
bright as day risen recast the gardens
took the journey to the West
and turning to me shone in my bed.

A: Send me the pillow that you dream on
one more time: those old numbers never let us be.
The Songs of the South, The Classic Anthology
Defined by Confucius, Nashville's plaints & pleas.

K: It was a country song broke his heart,
I say his heart but perhaps it was an echo chamber
vulnerable to any passing lilt: Oh Hank, why oh why
d'you say that about the way and not the way.

A: Even in Nashville the way that can be told
is not the constant way. Chang E knew it.
Perhaps it was her whispery lament double-tracked
or with lunar echo that broke Hank's heart.

K: It was the moon sat on the lonesome highway,
nothing could shift it, not magic herbs or love.
There's no way around it, said the zinger.
The moon on the lonesome highway big as life.

A: The ex-colonists tell tales in the Veterans Club,
okay they were lonesome but what times they had.
Above their heads Yi's trophies look sadly tarnished,
the pix of Chang E in bra & knickers faded long ago.

K: So what, that was in a foreign place over there
and besides the bint is banjoed – but for the moon
calling us out that night and little Johnny sobbing,
to be honest we crawled away in the mud, slick like.

1.3

'In the sixteenth century human life was disordered and talent stultified by the obsession of theology; today we are plague-stricken by politics.'

— Evelyn Waugh, *When the Going was Good*

A: There's a plague-pit round the corner from
the House of Commons called Tothill Fields where
Scotsmen press-ganged by King Charles were dumped
not killed by the Pest but at the Battle of Worcester.

K: When Christopher Hill invented real history
dumb politicians stopped reading it,
went for posh Business Studies and Law
though I can show you bullet holes in Banbury.

A: That the world might turn upside down yet again –
or just sideways – even RC converts couldn't imagine.
The obsession of theology never goes away. Nor plague.
Politics might – in Aristotle's sense – but not politicians.

K: Popular that year above all autobiographies,
The Paint-By-Numbers Plague Pit Guide.
Just as well, Eng-a-land had no friends, near or far.
Reportedly, Eng-a-land had grown tired of experts.

A: The Eng-a-lish boast they love tradition.
Government by fools has always served them.
Once they had a king called Nuncle
and Nuncle kept a fool who was a wise one.

K: After the Lollards, the Diggers and the Co-op,
the man from Nuncle made us fear our own shadows;
the world never went tapsalteerie
and the fool was told to kennel his dog.

A: Bad boy Bonzo flipped. He chewed up
his master's collection of *Socialist Workers*,
sicked himself on *Big Issues*. Jumped
his kennel, yelped down to the food bank.

K: Mayhew never wrote an allegory of the poor,
so Bonzo would be just chewing pulp.
Hey boy, sick it up for the preterite to eat.
All the members of the Social Mobility Commission have resigned.

A: Bonzo does as he's told but the preterite might
not fancy this regurgitated poster saying
'These bastards would love to fuck each other'
with accompanying photos of Thatcher & Blair.

K: Imagine their offspring: no need, forgive me,
take a turn from Tothill Fields, there they are,
in their constructive ambiguity, their paltering:
the Big Ben ding-dong replaced by Bonzo's barking.

A: 'Ordure! Ordure!' cries Mr Speaker
and the day does come when a grown man's proud
to weep in public. Call the scaffolders in
before a wicked wind puffs Big Ben into the plague-pit.

K: They forge their tears into brittle medals
and by rote award them to one another,
blow their trumpets on the wind of no-change;
annealing my heart for all the world to see.

A: They forge and forget although it's there in Hansard
if you can tear yourself away from the latest instalment
of Bonzo's 'Memoirs' – oh I see you can't,
you've got to where he stands alone against Europe.

K: He was told that night in the only language he knew:
your country, Eng-a-land, has played itself out,
the hills folded into themselves a miracle of green;
no those feet did not: this is the anti-Jerusalem.

A: 'Gimme another dose of simultaneous translation,
lemme check the facts' – Down, boy, down –
we're going for a good long walk on those clouded hills,
we'll gaze on Shard & Gherkin & burning gold.

K: And we're not coming back: made mighty again
by shrinkage and penury? No-one will vote for that,
nor walk backwards into the pit to Castle Bouncy:
'and wilt thou take the ape for thy counsellor?'

1.4

Since the early graves contained little or no provision for keeping the sand away from the body, this dryness had a remarkable effect on the preservation of the burial, the corpse becoming desiccated very rapidly after interment . . . It may be that seeing the still life-like bodies of the dead was the origin of the Egyptian belief in a continued existence . . . '

— A. J. Spencer, *Death in Ancient Egypt*

K: The chemistry of sand has a lot to answer for,
the little poets lined up, metaphors and banjos to hand,
plucking out a history of ideas launched on the Khamsin:
the stench of faithful pork thus borne tickles the nose.

A: I smell seered flesh but it's not Black Pig's.
According to the poets Black Pig's immortal.
According to the poets all the gods play banjo
and life & death are two sides of one illusion.

K: Above ground in the light Greeks ignored the mistake
but the Medici repackaged it for the Renaissance,
then bankrolled the industrial revolution and Netflix:
this is a brief overview for future study.

A: What else could we do in this hell-hive?
We read night and day, mostly rubbish but aloud
for company's sake: that's not singing you hear,
just the drone of the drones, tone-deaf.

K: The ethical options seem narrow, convergent;
company is good, though night went on all day:
we are waiting for Richard Rorty to arrive,
we are reaching out for a rational mythology.

A: We are reaching out for a better broken mirror
    but we still crave fascinating facts about Egypt
    e.g. every pharoah had a stillborn twin brother
    because duality in those days meant quality.

K: Thus began the two-for-one market tease.
    I think Redface has snuck across from Far Province,
    looking here, skipping there, eyes fixed
    doing the plural swivel and a mating yelp.

A: Redface knows a bargain when he sees one,
    food a weary shopper never wanted
    flung on some dilapidated grave for a hungry ghost.
    'Ghosts be damned', smirks Redface, spitting shrink-wrap.

K: It's a dark moment in the history of commerce;
    cheek by jowl – jackals, hawks and scarabs hold sway.
    Get back in the box you heraldic beasts;
    who put you in charge in the first place?

A: The man from Recycling sent us down here,
    the one who calls us his slaves because
    or so he says that fine custom's back in fashion –
    'yet another thing', he chortles, 'Marx did not foresee'.

K: Proletarian means you sell your kids into slavery,
    making the classical world great again by immiseration;
    there's more than one way to destroy Palmyra,
    more than one way to zero the contract of the living.

A: In 1955 George Thomson wrote as if
    the dictatorship of the proletariat
    was well advanced. Exactly where
    he didn't say although he quite liked Stalin.

K: Uncle Joe knew where back in '53,
it killed him and he took to the lecture circuit.
The god stands blank and unblinking in Gori,
removed in 2010 reinstatement requested 2012.

A: Either Uncle Joe spoilt the view from the town hall
or this was yet another case of spontaneous compunction,
allowance made for some slippage, of statues from pedestals or
of common usage: 'bourgeois' now a token of mild disapproval.

K: The little poets lined up, balalaikas to hand;
krasivaya said Mandelstam, recalling a red face
recalling Armenia, a land of real things and rivers.
Oh get back in your cartouche, said the General Secretary.

A: Scroll out your copy of the Book of the Dead,
the personalised one – your second mortgage, remember?
Search until you realise your place, dry as dry gets,
its ceiling bedecked with your stars of choice.

2.1

'By the middle of the ninth century Baghdad's mills produced enough paper for
the use of all the secretaries and administrators in the War Office, the Office of
Expenditure, the State Treasury, the Office of Correspondence, the Office of Letter
Opening, the Caliphal Bank and the Post and Intelligence Office. [...] More than a
hundred shops selling paper and books lined the Stationers' Market in the south-
west of the city.'

— Rebecca Stott, *Darwin's Ghosts*

A: I reckon you've been missing some sleep, Jāḥiẓ,
    ever since you bought those 19 vols of whatshisname,
    Aristotle? Now you're heading for the mosque
    to wise up the wise, tonight out catching desert flies.

K: Aristotle my friend, identified a category mistake,
    called it the application of an alien name – forget status;
    masque for mosque, trade for raid, Khurasan for Kardashian:
    markets, the House of Wisdom, all that sherbet, comes next.

A: I'll offer your rhymes to Abū Nuwās
    when he's sobered up. He's still in the winebar,
    says the dawn muezzin doesn't mean last orders.
    His category mistake's not telling boys from girls.

K: Huh that bad man, comes of all that reading,
    the souse sloshing the wine and scribbling post-fuck;
    just saying his name will land me on a watch list,
    Abū Nuwās wired his saz, invented rock and roll.

A: You can't move in this god-gifted place without meeting
someone inventing something. The lamp's alight in
al-Khwārizmī's window, he'll be at his quadratics,
compendiously calculating Hindu methods of completion.

K: For all that we inherited numerical zero
we began with nothing and kept most of it;
across Madīnat as-Salām earthly lights flicker
a thousand thoughts, the work of delight, of seeing.

A: The perfect circle of a city signifying peace.
Cf. Plato's Atlantis in the recent translation.
Cf. the map of the eye with crystalline lens dead centre.
Cf. the Ingenious Instrument which Sounds by Itself.

K: The eye is that part of the brain uncovered
and there may be a thinking centre;
there are the terraces of Dioce shining
and those are the colours of the stars.

A: I've read that this was in the land of Nod and the poet
was dreaming of the city Cain founded. Where Daniel
the prophet according to Josephus built his palace.
In another account: centre everywhere thought nowhere.

K: Well it would help if the rule here applied elsewhere,
you have to have your name on your door
said the postman, carrying instructions to Cain
on how to bury that head in the foundations of the city.

A: The same postman who trousered the Baghdad cheque
Cain was meant to bury with the head & other bric-a-brac,
panther skins, ostrich feathers, dirty banned verses etc.;
who said Your door isn't numbered, unlike your days.

K: According to Lévi-Strauss there's a corpse under every city.
    Who killed my brother? I did said the word with my gift for abstraction.
    According to Claude the prophet, that's the rot in everything,
    the pervasive stench in all our civilised dealings – but I doubt it.

A: Although you can't ignore the stench. Maybe it's
    bad drains that bring cities down, sewers built
    for less shit and fewer words, before broken
    promises and fatbergs increased in direct proportion.

K: Oh you and the irreducible exotica of empire,
    everyone here carries a connection back to those times;
    the learning unpacked with bullet holes in the saddlebag,
    a splash of light in the face of resurgent darkness.

A: Algorithms rule OK but when it comes to
    fatbergs there's nothing for it but picks and drills,
    for dictators rockets and firebombs: pretend
    Saddam wasn't our man, set up for a purpose.

K: He wore a fine Kevlar bonnet, our man from Takrit
    stocked a library full of Stalin but kept it quite discrete;
    my friends my writ's the lesser of two evils, he said,
    yes he was a useful brute but then we hanged him dead.

2.2

'Numbers stations are believed to be the encrypted transmissions of secret services like MI5, the CIA and Mossad to their agents in the field.'

> — Akin Fernandez, BBC Radio 4, Tracking The Lincolnshire Poacher, Simon Fanshawe, 2005.

K: I heard her voice, I heard distance and atmospherics,
   the harmonics a brittle calculation filling the air,
   the momentary architecture of Eurydice's dark signal;
   If you name me I'm taken. And the message? *Act now.*

A: Yes the voice was female but the static so bad
   in seconds she was gone. Then knock knock on the door.
   Quick switch to medium wave, the Light Programme,
   Mister 'Orne & a shiny night in the season of the year.

K: Under occupation in Lesser Johnsonia we wept,
   or laughed, at such in-character antics, a comedy folksong
   by Twisting Michael of the Gove and Vladimir, Prince of Data;
   02588 02588 91326 91326 – said it all, an absolute classic.

A: If you can't guess how the first two 2's explain
   the second 6 I'd call you dead meat. Live meat's no better
   but it's no use standing by the mirror, fag between fingers,
   as cocksure as Philby just after he'd been cleared.

K: I was listening to the radio in another country
   skewered off centre, that sort of displacement,
   you live with it but don't, like swimming, like pretending;
   flash-bulb poetry goes pop, changes nothing.

A: It always comes back to the meaning of numbers,
    counting syllables, stress, puzzling where you dropped
    your one-time pad with this week's key: on your knees,
    elbow-deep in the waste-paper basket, Sir Clueless.

K: It comes back to reading *Ulysses* for one word
    Under the Volcano for another and Beckett for a comma.
    I should have paid more attention in prac crit,
    the meaning of numbers dancing in the world.

A: To break the pentameter a century ago
    and now the casaPound thugs shout they'll rescue
    Il Duce from his lamppost, set him loose again.
    Let me count the ways to celebrate a poet.

K: One way is by having friends in high/low places:
    though Angleton couldn't make a poem stand up
    he saw E Pound through his stickiest moment
    and then founded the CIA dot dash dot dash etc.

A: Angleton had more friends than liquid lunches, that's
    saying something. Plied with drinks by – here he is again,
    Kim Philby. Wasn't Angleton paranoid enough? Dashing
    into Kasper's bookstore for the latest Square Dollar.

K: The convergence of poetry and espionage was a curious thing.
    Whoever thought there was influence in verses? Forget it Bonzo;
    big data, Cambridge Analytica – it's not a post-Prynne school,
    as if the privileged sons of England would ever trade in betrayal.

A: How many things Cambridge stands for, even Apostles.
    One numbers station switched to broadcasting poems
    cognoscenti decode as Mao's words from the grave.
    How many things only Cambridge will stand for.

K: I know I know, their brains went tick tick
and there once was a city on the eastern edge
of a failing country where it all came down to numbers,
to break the century a parameter ago.

A: As soon as there's a number for everything
it's the dread of Pythagoras: nothing adds up.
You tell yourself you're you because your ID says so
but your soul's dear seat's reduced to a SIM card.

K: Around the lamppost the dimwit rascals ran,
they did the light programme skitter dance,
the square number dance, the forget-her-voice twist;
but no-one moved the rocks, trees or gentle beasts.

A: No-one including Angleton, convinced of
the Monster Plot, sacked at last for his conviction.
Ah let's twist again like we did last summer.
Let's not let up: twisting time's still here.

2.3

'[Robin Dunbar] argues that language evolved [...] initially as a supplement to grooming, and then as a replacement for it.'

– Steven Mithen, *The Prehistory of the Mind*

A: The Sphinx asked another question: 'what both
    saves & wastes time?' Oedipus, stumped, sat glumly
    brushing Jocasta's hair. 'I think the answer's Talk'
    she whispered but Oedipus never would listen.

K: Oedipus, like most of us, heard but didn't listen,
    even in the language lab, headphones clamped on;
    in the tunnels of being, Jocasta, Iocasta, Io, grief or joy,
    Shining Moon or Woe-Adorned: use your ears fool.

A: Day after day, the whole bloody winter,
    nitpicking all week then laying down the law.
    In our language we have 28 words for the moon
    and thirteen times as many for headlice.

K: According to Rorty it's our job alone
    to send sparkling metaphor into mundanity
    so others see the river's mouth and what Marx meant;
    I wonder, let's sit on the bank and sing or else.

A: Or go buy a one-way ticket to Babylon or
    somewhere everything's so utterly unlike another thing
    all you can do with a towel is throw it in,
    sit and wait for the next dose of liberation.

K: I could say the slow syntax of her fingertips on my back
spelt out there's a place for us somewhere, spelt out
the world falls through the crack in every metaphor
but special pleading gets you nowhere and another thing.

A: There are cracks and cracks, some you can fly through
like a shaman's smokehole. Or could. Back when.
Before critical mass and the massage parlour.
The new syntax, new sentence, new new that isn't news.

K: Shaman drove the bus – eyes closed of course,
the bus was called the Next Dose of Liberation.
The bus broke down on the metaphor tour,
the journey narrated in non-refundable language.

A: That old bone-rattler – look at Shaman now,
arms & legs torn off, arse wrapped round his ears.
Putting him together again's the H.Dumpty problem,
all those liberated words re-defined as he pleases.

K: Gather the limbs, ears and other parts into a bag,
reset those original terms to first inscription;
facts are only facts if I agree them, the dead walk,
and remember, there's no history unless I say so.

A: You need to stroke history behind the ears
and tickle its tummy to make history talk.
Then watch how those bones re-articulate,
skull puffing up like a hot air balloon.

K: Them bones do rattle and they are for keeping,
we have 28 terms for the endless language issue,
every one of them bores me into torpid submission;
radiant bones in X-ray having the last laugh.

A: 'So', says Shaman, 'you've seen through yourself.
At last. So now you can watch my skeleton dance,
hear my dry bones sing. So when language issues
through a pillar of smoke you won't see through me'.

K: The human frame articulated a second thought,
if you'll just lie still the picture's made from sound;
tell the spooks such truth sings without the autotune,
I think that was the thing that we were given.

A: Hymnbooks in hand they came to bury Shaman,
sang the one about Time's ever-rolling stream,
shovelled dictionaries & lexicons in with the soil.
None guessed they'd all guessed the coffin was empty.

K: And with that there was nothing left to say
said the rocks, the river, the mouldering books,
said the shovel, the language of bliss, the smoke;
so Iocasta blinked and sought a second thought.

2.4

'The inhabitants of Britain who live on the promontory called Belerion are especially friendly to strangers and have adopted a civilised way of life because of their interaction with traders and other people.'

– Diodorus Siculus, *Bibliotheca Historica.*

K: With the first candid dawn over breaking water
　　we came to an island off an island out of rumour;
　　our ship hit the rocks of a commensurate metaphor.
　　Well the way we normally do things here. You. Me. That.

A: So populous a country, such a crowd on that beach,
　　the wreck stripped before noon but kindly done.
　　We were signed up the cliff, drank their sugary brew,
　　admired their brooches & earrings of rare white metal.

K: Abacus in one hand, knife in the other – you choose.
　　So we clambered the hill horizon, expecting a city,
　　there was none, only dogs, huts and smelting;
　　their technê, a pivot, turned the world upside down.

A: How describe a city to people who've never
　　heard of an agora – or forum – or walked down a street?
　　When we called a house a three-storey hut
　　their laughter might have landed in their faerie kingdom.

K: How describe Hippodamian principles?
　　Each citizen the same plot and access to the gods;
　　where will it all end? – the Fabian Society?
　　It's called a customs union: you me that.

A: Imagine, a council of lawless lawyers,
    fruit-juice addicts swapping God for Eros,
    all citizens to wear home-made sandals:
    Back to Belerion & Back to Nature.

K: That was the season of online hysteria
    home-made scandals and political ineptitude;
    the etymology king issued edicts for first meanings
    rode his dog Foolish backwards in the market.

A: I remember that king in his madness, no Lear
    but convinced he was James Nayler sent from Heaven
    to save us. Never one to let a quibble pass him by.
    'Politics? Ineptitude?' he'd snap. 'Same thing.'

K: Well we're bound by tautology, that stout rope
    knotted at the ankle, cranking us down to hell
    or nothing, even the show of ape world gone;
    the ground stuffed with kings, sane and otherwise.

A: If you were a king in the isles of Britain
    with your head embalmed in oil of cedar
    dangling from the neck of a horse Dio Sic
    reckons you'd think differently of rope.

K: It makes my neck itch, that thought
    and their ways remain strange even to this day;
    also embalmed, a squalid orientation holds sway
    – Who can we turn our backs on next?

A: White hetero men, grey squirrels, bad badgers,
    French manufacturers of British passports,
    an endless hate list's the birthright & privilege
    of all most fortunate members of an island race.

K: One day we'll all be sent back to where we came from
and the country will be empty and there will be nothing,
just the pretty hills and paltering, a political class
running in fear of the heart-felt bigotry of a lost tribe.

A: I-den-ti-ty I-den-ti-ty's the game they play
in the poetry workshops and political classrooms.
I watched them jog & jot first memories as Teacher told them;
fancied origins, original fancies, fit ghost-town graffiti.

K: The thing is – I don't care who you are nor who I am,
the goods from those workshops fail before reaching port:
thus embalmed heads go yip yip, shrink and blanche;
remember – strangers are sent through the world by god.

A: That's what the miners told us, they who
never referred to their god by name. Perhaps
called Kilroy as scribbled on boghouse walls,
perhaps the shrunken heads revealed it: Yip Yip.

www.ingramcontent.com/pod-product-compliance
Lightning Source LLC
Chambersburg PA
CBHW050258090426
42734CB00027B/3499